MOTSWANA: AFRICA, DREAM AGAIN

MOTSWANA: AFRICA, DREAM AGAIN

a play by Donald Molosi

THE MANTLE

New York

THE MANTLE
21-33 36th St.
Queens, NY 11105
mantlebooks.com | @TheMantle

CONTENTS

PRODUCTION HISTORY

Motswana: Africa, Dream Again was first performed on November 17, 2012 at the United Solo Festival, the world's largest solo theatre festival, in New York City. It was presented as a solo play written, directed, and performed by Donald Molosi.

Motswana premiered in Botswana in late 2013 as a two-hander starring Donald Molosi in one of the roles. Since then, the play has been performed across North America. In 2015, *Motswana* toured Botswana and South Africa and returned to the United Solo Festival for an encore performance.

AWARDS

In March 2013, *Motswana* was selected for online publication by Indie Theater Now, a prestigious online database of plays. The play has been reviewed in *The New York Theater Review* and other prestigious Broadway publications.

PLAYWRIGHT'S NOTE

For obvious reasons, nation states usually promote only a singular streamlined national identity of themselves, thus neglecting the story of said nation's heterogeneity. In *Motswana: Africa, Dream Again* though, I wanted to explore the somewhat homogenous national identity of Botswana through the stories of Botswana's own ethnic diversity. *Motswana* discusses not the cohesiveness of a nation but the points of slippage, where intranational diversity implodes and exposes the limitations of the umbrella concept of a nation, and whether one can truly come from a nation if a nation is an unfixed idea. Nations are constructs; they expand and contract, and sometimes disappear.

"Motswana" simply means "citizen of Botswana." The Republic of Botswana is often called Africa's golden example for its enduring democracy and relative wealth. This multilayered multilingual play satirically and docu-dramatically asks:

1) Who, exactly, can confidently claim to be a Motswana?

2) What unexpected revelations about the Motswana identity surface once we acknowledge that African borders were fabricated not in aid of the cohesion of African nations but to serve colonialism?

3) Given the migratory nature of African peoples before the invention of borders on the continent, is "Motswana" a misnomer for describing Botswana nationals?

Parts of the script are adapted from actual speeches by President Thabo Mbeki, Philly Lutaaya, and President Seretse Khama. Yvonne Vera's work on Chaminuka and Nehanda also inspired certain parts.

***

This play is dedicated to my dear mother, Gosego Nnananyana Molosi, who is my ultimate Motswana.

—Donald Molosi
Gaborone, Botswana
October, 2015

CAST OF CHARACTERS

PAPA/TIMOTHY ZIBANANI GULUBANI: Patriarch of the Gulubani family. He is in his sixties. He is a conservative politician who earned his wealth from a long political career.

MAMA/CECILIA GULUBANI: Matriarch of the Gulubani family. She is in her early fifties and is a devoted mother and wife. She does not enjoy her job at the office.

BOEMO GULUBANI: Thirty-year-old man with unconventional ideas. He is a Member of Parliament and lives with his parents.

UNCLE TSHEKEDI: Seretse Khama's uncle and guardian. He is in his forties and is both a disciplinarian and a devout Christian.

SERETSE KHAMA: Founding President of Botswana. In this play he's portrayed at age 27. He is passionate, diplomatic, and visionary.

CHAMINUKA: The ancestral spirit who visits to avenge his fellow Africans against colonizers. His age is timeless.

NEHANDA: The ancestral spirit who visits to avenge her fellow Africans. This is the spirit-wife of Chaminuka. Her age is timeless.

PHILLIP "PHILLY" LUTAAYA: He is the first African to declare he has AIDS. He is portrayed in this play at age 38.

NOTES ON SET DESIGN AND COSTUMES

The non-English lines must be performed as written in the script alongside the English. Simple costume changes are recommended in transition between characters. Live music on the guitar and/ or drums is also recommended. Although this play was initially presented as a solo play, it may be performed with more actors as an ensemble piece.

MOTSWANA: AFRICA, DREAM AGAIN

by
Donald Molosi

How can I come from a nation?
How can a human being come from a concept?
—Taiye Selasi

Scene 1: These Young Generations

Upbeat Botswana music begins to play. As lights come up, Mama is already on stage setting the table. Papa enters. He is older and he walks with a limp. Papa and Mama are about to have supper.

PAPA: Cecilia my wife, I have been telling you, eh? This son of ours is what? Too much. Hmm...

(Pause.)

What is with this daft generation and their questions, anyway? Did questions ever fill any man's stomach? Do questions not just pour water onto simmering fat? I say, gone are the days when children were manageable, and believed what you told them they were, full-stop!

(Pause.)

Boemo is too much.

(Mockingly imitating Boemo.) Heei, I am half Kalanga and half Ngwato! *Hei wee,* I am one quarter Shona and one eighth Xhosa! *Hei wee* this! *Hei wee* that! Nincompoop.

(Romantically reminiscing on the past.)

In my day you were told that you took your father's identity and that was that. None of this *matakala* and noise and debate.

(Actor sucks his teeth as Papa and then transforms into Mama. She is calm and at first sight she seems to be feminine in a quiet, traditional way.)

MAMA: Must you really be this outraged by it? Certainly you cannot deny that our son is all those things. At least we in this country are fortunate enough to know our ancestral history, unlike our brothers and sisters across the ocean.

PAPA: Eh-eh. Tell me *mmaabo,* what man would have a totem if we all chose to be so many things at once? Would the tribes not disappear? I beg. This is not a light matter, my wife.

(He takes a sip of his scotch.)

MAMA: *Ah, rraabo.* Let the boy be. *Ga ke re* to call oneself a Motswana is not to call oneself not-Zimbabwean, not-Namibian, not—

PAPA: Ah-ha! You agree with him?

(Calling out.) Gods! Even my own wife is testing me today? Kalanga Gods of Gulubani, do you hear my lamentations? *Heei!*

(Clapping hands theatrically.)

My wife, if I am hearing you correctly... you are confessing that Boemo's ideas are entering your head.

MAMA: *(Slightly amused by his melodrama.)* Do lower your voice, my husband. Boemo might hear you from his room.

(Reasoning with him.) Listen, you must cool your head before anything can be solved. As our fathers say, no matter how hot your anger is, it cannot cook a potato.

(Crosses to him.)

Now listen, father of my children. I am only trying to tell you what you already know, which is the fact that our ancestors moved freely across all these savannas. All these lakes. All these hills. Why then would what Boemo says be strange?

PAPA: Eh-eh! I refuse. What does that make me? Or you?

MAMA: Who knows? I am just saying that the new generation might not be altogether nonsensical.

PAPA: This is too much. I mean, does Boemo think he is the boss of us? Does he actually think that he—

Hmm...

Colossians 3:20 says, "Children, obey your parents in every-thing, for this PLEASES THE LORD!" Yet my son's questions continue to rub mud in my face.

MAMA: The same bible that demonizes your Gods of Gulubani, eh?

PAPA: *(Long pause. Papa sighs.)* Let us eat our supper in peace, my wife.

(Lights fade.)

Scene 2: Ode to Thabo Mbeki

Atmospheric percussion plays. Boemo rises from the ground as though sprouting from the earth like a seed. He speaks with feeling and with a slow urgency. Throughout the play, Boemo speaks out loud while scribbling in his journal.

BOEMO: I am an African. At the same time I am a Motswana. I owe my being to the hills and the valleys, the mountains and the glades, the rivers, the deserts, the trees, the flowers, the seas, and the ever-changing seasons that define the face of our native land.

My body has frozen in our frosts and in our snows. It has thawed in the warmth of our sunshine and melted in the heat of the midday sun. The crack and the rumble of the summer thunders, lashed by startling lightning, have been a cause of both trembling and hope. Nature's fragrances have been as pleasant to us as the sight of blooming flowers.

The dramatic shapes of the Drakensberg, the soil-colored waters of the Okavango, the perennial Zambezi, and the time-less sands of the Kgalagadi are all panels on the natural stage where we act out the theatre of our day.

At times, and in fear, I have wondered whether I should concede equal citizenship of our countries to the leopard and the lion, the elephant and the springbok, the hyena, the black mamba, and the pestilential mosquito, for there exists a human presence among all these. A feature on the face of our native land thus defined. I know that none dare challenge me when I say, I am an African.

I owe my being to the Khoi and the San, Basarwa of the seventeenth century whose desolate souls stalk the great expanses of the beautiful Cape, haunt the epic Chinoyi Caves, and march the majestic Makgadikgadi. They who fell victim to the most merciless genocide our native land has ever seen. They who were the first to lose their lives in the struggle to defend our freedom and independence. Like the Hottentot Venus.

PAPA: Son, do you mean Saartjie Baartman?

BOEMO: Yes.

(Regaining his thought.)

They who were first to lose their lives in the struggle to defend our freedom and independence. Like Saartjie Baartman, whom the French exhibited in a cage like a wild animal. Ota Benga, whom the Americans exhibited in a New York City zoo as a specimen of an African pygmy until he could no longer bear the humiliation and took his own life. El Negro de Banyoles, the Mothaping King whose body the French exhumed, eviscerated, and stuffed in the same way as a trophy animal and then gave to a Spanish museum to exhibit.

Today, as a people, we are audibly silent about these ancestors, fearful to admit the horror of a former deed, seeking to obliterate from our memories a cruel occurrence, burying our histories with the bones of our ancestors.

(Pause.)

I am formed of the Tswana people who ruled the land between

the Okavango and the Vaal rivers. I am formed of the Kalangas ba-ka Nswazwi, of Mujaji the Rain Queen. I am formed of migrants who left Europe to find a new home on our native land. Whatever their actions, they remain part of me.

In my veins courses the blood of the Malay slaves who came from the East. Their proud dignity informs my bearing, their culture a part of my essence. The stripes they bore on their bodies from the lash of the slave master are a reminder embossed on my consciousness of what should not be done.

I am the grandchild of the warrior men and women led by Kgosi Khama and Kgosi Sechele, the patriots that Mbuya Nehanda and Sekuru Kaguvi took to battle, the soldiers that Kgosi Moshoeshoe and King Shaka Zulu—

PAPA: Son, do you mean Nkosi Shaka Zulu?

BOEMO: Yes. The soldiers that Kgosi Moshoeshoe and Nkosi Shaka Zulu taught never to dishonor the cause of freedom.

(Beat.)

My mind and my knowledge of myself are formed by the victories that are the jewels in our African crowns, the victories we earned from Lagos to Juba, from Dimawe to Sophiatown, as the Ashanti of Ghana, as the Berbers of the Sahara, as the Swahili of Tanganyika. Being part of all these people, and in the knowledge that none dare contest that assertion, I shall claim that I am an African. And I am a Motswana.

Scene 3: State of the Nation

Papa and Mama. This time they are not eating but doing different actions around the house. She is absent-mindedly reading a newspaper while watching television and occasionally flicking through channels. Papa is opening mail with a letter opener and occasionally pauses to skim the letters.

MAMA: *Ijaa!* The news these days! Why is it on the front page that a cabinet minister slept with two young women at the same time?

(Looking up from the newspaper and pausing to look at the TV.) Is this news? They are showing that plump beauty queen again? Someone tell me what I am looking at.

PAPA: I tell you these days all things are tumbling into rough weather.

(Laughing.) Look at her chew her tongue, this professed beauty queen. The girl threatens to fall asleep mid-sentence. *(Laughing some more.)*

MAMA: Is this beauty?

PAPA: She is a dunderhead! Nincompoops. All of them. I shit upon such radicalism.

MAMA: *(Looking at her newspaper.)* Really, how about they put Motsamai Mpho on the front page? He founded this republic and even named it. And now he just died and there is barely any mention of—

PAPA: My wife, gone are the days of good journalism. The days of Rampholo Molefhe. Russ Molosiwa. Those were the days. Sometimes I think that after the British left we plunged into mediocrity.

MAMA: *(Showing Papa a newspaper article.)* And look at this, they mistakenly published Kenneth Kaunda's eulogy while he is still alive!

PAPA: Nincompoops.

MAMA: *(Smacking the newspaper.)* And this woman is dancing around in her panties telling people that she has sexual desires for President Ian Khama. I am finished with this newspaper!

PAPA: People these days love to read about decay. Ignoramuses.

These media are the reason our son Boemo maintains this foolish talk of having ancestors across our borders. This kind of chatter enrages me. Gods, did I not send him to English Medium schools? Yet, he disgraces me.

MAMA: Come off it, *rraabo*. Perhaps no one will even read his bloody memoir.

PAPA: This boy will lose his seat in Parliament. I repeat, *mmaabo*, a fly that does not listen follows the dead body into the grave.

MAMA: Ah-ah, no more! We are not talking about that boy again, my husband.

(Mama opens the display unit to take out special wine glasses. She takes out a bottle of wine from the fridge.)

At least this whole business makes him curious about history.

(Smiling.) Anyway, my handsome husband, let us enjoy this Sunday afternoon with a nice splash of chardonnay.

PAPA: *(Pulls a gift from under the sofa and gives it to her. Pause.)* Happy anniversary, my wife.

MAMA: *(Gleeful.)* You remembered? Happy anniversary, Zibanani, father of my children.

(They kiss.)

PAPA: Genesis 2:24. "Therefore a man shall leave his father and his mother and hold fast to his wife, and they shall become one flesh." You are still all I could dream of, my beautiful mermaid.

MAMA: Twenty-six years.

PAPA: Yes. And still going so strong.

MAMA: *(She sings a verse from a Shania Twain song she likes, "You're Still The One." She sings pretty well. She gets a little theatrical with her gestures and moves with the song, but her sincerity is true. After a couple of lines of singing a cappella, the live musician joins in with guitar.)*

Ain't nothin' better. We beat the odds together. I'm glad we didn't listen. Look at what we would be missin'. They said, "I bet they'll never make it." But just look at us holdin' on. We're still together, still goin' strong. You're still the one I run to. The one that I belong to. You're still the one I want for life.

(She has a little giggle fit and takes a mock bow. He claps.)

Zibanani, do you remember our poem from our first anniversary in Serowe?

PAPA: Of course.

MAMA: *(Teasing him.) Kana,* you used to be romantic.

(Shooing him teasingly when he tries to embrace her.)

Ah, leave me. *Ija,* do you even remember that sweet-sweet poem?

PAPA: *(Pause, and then he begins to recite. Perhaps, a little strumming on the guitar in the background.)*

Chobe, Gcwihaba, and the Linyanti—all of them ethereal, *moratiwa.* Beauteous and timeless.

MAMA: From the Tswapong Hills to the sands of Struizendam— all of them ethereal, *moratiwa*: beauteous and timeless.

PAPA: Still my favorite place in Botswana is in this marriage with you. *Ndokuda.*

MAMA: *Ke a go rata.*

PAPA: Prayerfully do we recite this, therefore that we may grow old together like a folktale and its lesson.

MAMA: That we may hold steadfastly onto this marriage the way that Bangwato proudly hold onto Serowe.

(They kiss.)

Scene 4: Motswana

Upbeat Botswana music begins to play as the actor changes into Boemo.

BOEMO: Place of birth? The town of Mahalapye, central Botswana. Full name? Boemo Timothy Gulubani. Height? One meter, 64 centimeters. Nationality? Motswana. That is what my passport says.

Motswana. It is a word used to refer to someone one belonging to one of the Tswana ethnic groups like Bakwena, Bangwaketse, Bangwato, and others—they are all Tswana people with totems ranging from crocodile to duiker to buffalo. But since these Tswana groups form the majority in the Republic of Botswana, every citizen in the country has to refer to themselves nationally as a "Motswana." How can we be stress-free about this issue? I have to call myself by that word, Motswana, a word that defines the country only by its ethnic majority. That is the very sand in my porridge; I have to call myself by this word that denies my father's ethnicity. We must not season this bitter issue with sweet lies and so I shall speak.

My father's side is Kalanga, definitely not a Tswana group. Totems there range from birds to animal hearts to whetstone. As I wrote in the previous chapter, my mother's side is Ngwato and therefore Tswana. But—according to some— since a child always takes the ethnicity of the father, I am not then ethnically a Motswana. This is no small madness!

Motswana is part of myself and, like stagnant water, I cannot run from myself. But instead of keeping a bruised silence, I often wonder out loud what would happen to that word, Motswana, if we imagined the southern African region without borders. Would the land not bloom with mobile citizens and fecund consciousnesses?

I always conclude that I could own that term—Motswana—only if I choose to see it as a diaspora, a more elastic and more inclusive identity: as a people that lie in the still-colonial territory I was born in as well as on the outskirts, in the so-called "neighboring countries" and so-called "other countries." That definition of Motswana does not cough out my Kalanga ancestry, you see. That understanding of the word ensures that everyone within these borders can have a hero. That is the Motswana that no one can Other.

Let me start with my mother's side, the Tswana side. She comes from the Bangwato ethnic group, the largest ethnic group in Botswana, one of the several in the country that can rightfully call themselves ethnically Motswana. Interestingly, Bangwato were the first Botswana ethnic group to approve of an interracial marriage when, in 1948, their King Seretse Khama married a white English woman, Ruth Williams, in London. King Seretse's guardian, Prince Tshekedi Khama, was opposed to the marriage and asked Seretse to return home from England to justify his unusual proposal before the entire ethnic group. And when, on November 13, 1948, the Bangwato accepted this interracial marriage and welcomed the prospect of mixed-blood royals, the definition of Motswana, as far as I am concerned, was immediately made elastic in a new way. It was expanded beyond race.

(Traditional Botswana guitar music begins to play.)

Scene 5: Seretse Khama

The following scene begins with a correspondence by telegram between Seretse Khama and his Uncle Tshekedi. "STOP" denotes the punctuation in a telegram. It can be said out loud in performance or omitted as the director chooses.

TSHEKEDI: My dear Sonny, sending you this telegram hoping

you arrived safely in London (STOP) Everything well in Serowe (STOP) Your uncle and father, Tshekedi Khama

SERETSE: Dear Uncle, settling well in England. Feeling lonely sometimes. Not enjoying courses in Latin and Greek (STOP) Changing degree to Law. Your nephew and son, Seretse

TSHEKEDI: My dear Sonny, congratulations on settling well (STOP) May my brother's spirit protect you his beloved son (STOP) Put work into studies and be successful at the end of the year (STOP) Law is good choice for future leader (STOP) Your uncle and father, Tshekedi Khama

(Long pause.)

SERETSE: Dear Uncle, I send greetings (STOP) Thank you for sending my allowances early (STOP) Happy to write with good news —

(Pause.)

Her name is Ruth Williams (STOP) Your nephew and son, Seretse Khama

TSHEKEDI: Dear Sonny, suspending your allowances (STOP) You are Prince of Bangwato (STOP) You are going to be chief (STOP) Your people cannot accept this (STOP) Formal signing of documents in England does not constitute your marriage, as far as we are concerned no marriage exists (STOP) We accept nothing short of dissolution of that marriage (STOP) Our decision firm (STOP) Welfare of tribe paramount in this case (STOP) Repeat: Formal signing of documents in England does not constitute your marriage (STOP) Your father, Tshekedi Khama

SERETSE: Dear Uncle, tribe and you important to me (STOP) But already married (STOP) Dissolution unacceptable (STOP) ready to return with wife (STOP) Suspension of allowances being felt (STOP) I pay four guineas weekly for my flat (STOP) *Ke le ngwana wa gago*, Seretse

TSHEKEDI: Dear Sonny, allowances sent (STOP) Airfare to Botswana (STOP) For one passenger (STOP) Get ready to leave at moment's notice (STOP) I can only discuss your proposal personally after your arrival here

("Bagammangwato Ba Ga Mabiletsa" or another song of the director's choice begins to play on guitar as actor puts on jacket to perform Seretse's justification of his marriage in Serowe, 1948.)

SERETSE: *Ke ne ke sa le todise matho bagolo mme ha le eletsa keka le rerisa gape ka ngwetsi ya lona*—am not bitter. But I am frustrated. Because I have been banned and I am compelled to live in England, to lead my people toward independence from abroad. *Rrangwane*, I have not yet been able to find out what I have done wrong.

(Increasing urgency.)

I have been told that my marriage is contrary to native custom, but I can prove that it is not!

(Pause. Seeking to reason with elders, he resorts to Setswana.)

Ka jalo ke ne ke kopa gore le mo amogele ka mabogo oo mabedi.

(Pause. Elders oppose the idea of this marriage.)

Bagolo bame, ga ke dirise—

(Elders cut him off and, to his surprise, they are more opposed than before.)

Ke a itse. I know. All I ask is that you accept her as my wife, as part of our royal family. I realize that I did not consult you about the engagement, yes.

(Pause.)

What does that mean, my elders? *Rrangwane* Tshekedi, just how will my divorce guarantee that we will claim our independence from the British?

(Pause, and then asking genuinely.)

What would the people, the Bangwato, have me do? It has been said that I am a coward and that I ought to say outright that I do not want to be chief, that my heart is not with you or with this protectorate. But I cannot say that; it is not in my thoughts and it is not so. I cannot say it just so that you will think that I am a man. You are angry with me because I will not leave my wife, a woman that you do not want. I cannot force you to accept her. I have admitted that I took her against your will and you have told me that you will not allow her to come here. You have the power to do that. If the power had been mine she would already be here. I love my country and my people and I have told you that even though there is this disagreement, I still want to be your chief. You say that because of her I cannot be your chief.

(Menacing, desperately.)

Were I to part from her today, become chief, and then take her up again tomorrow, you would not then tell me that I must leave the tribe. Then I would be on the throne and could do as I pleased. But I have not cheated you. I have given you this chance to rule me. You all say you do not want the woman *youdonotwantthewoman!*

I have told you, I tell you now. I cannot leave her, I cannot leave her. I cannot—

Scene 6: Across the Color Line

BOEMO: After that one event, the Motswana identity ceased to be about color. But that did not squash inequality.

My father's Kalangas are a minority in Botswana and their language is not taught in schools or used in journalism: in many ways they get the opposite treatment of what my mother's people get.

Whereas my mother's ethnically Tswana people are dominant in politics, my father's Kalanga people are not. While ethnically Tswana figures appear with smirking faces on every denomination of our pula, no Kalangas or non-ethnically-Tswana figures are recognized in the same way, despite their contributions to the creation and sustenance of this republic.

So, within the borders of Botswana, I am from both the dominant group as well as the subaltern. And thanks to our chronically colonized curriculum, I know little about the subaltern side. But I do know some things about the Kalangas' cousins, the Shona, who are mainly found in modern-day Zimbabwe. It seems, therefore, that to be a Motswana is to have those gaps in knowledge of one's roots, those silences.

We are told that when the Europeans came with the Bible in 1881 they sought to erase all religions that existed among my father's people. We are also told that that is when the spirit of Chaminuka found a medium in a man by the name of Pasipamire. The spirits of our ancestors spoke through him and in the process protected beliefs of all the people in the land, whether Shona, Ndebele, Tswana, or whatever else.

Like two peas in a pod, the spirit of Chaminuka is always accompanied by that of Nehanda. The story of Nehanda is always a reminder that the moment an African turns against another, our downfall is certain. Our condition is that delicate. Xenophobia should seem almost suicidal. More in the next chapter.

Scene 7: Ode to Yvonne Vera

Atmospheric music ushers in Chaminuka. The live musician says the shared lines with the actor, if the play is presented as a solo.

CHAMINUKA: I am the spirit Chaminuka. My God lives up above. He is a pool of water in the sky. My God is a rain-giver.

I approach my God through my ancestors and my *mudzimu*. I brew beer for my god to praise him, and I dance. Tell them that, child. What kind of god is theirs that he will not be appeased with beer poured onto the ground?

CHAMINUKA AND NEHANDA: Chosen child, do they even know that if they killed you a patch of grass as large as your head would appear on the ground where you would then fall forward and join us? Do they?

CHAMINUKA: Agitator of the magnificent downfall of the Barozwi and the Matebele! Spirit of the proud land between the rivers of Limpopo and Zambezi! I AM CHAMINUKA! Owner of the land, commander of the wind! I know everything and nothing is impossible to me!

Tell them, child, that I, Chaminuka the great spirit of our lions, rivers, and caves never wanted this peculiar god who is inside their book. They tell us that in heaven we shall not labor. Why would a man long for that kind of happiness? Work is not suffering; it is not punishment for a man to do all he can for a good solid harvest. For a man not to labor is contemptible laziness. Shall we go to heaven to be lazy? To sit behind our huts and bask in the sun like lizards?

Scene 8: Holy Nehanda

Atmospheric music ushers in Nehanda.

NEHANDA: Who is this coming from the hills, from Chidamba, with her garments stained crimson?

CHAMINUKA AND NEHANDA: Who is this, robed in splendor, striding forward in the greatness of her eternity? *Nditaurire aniko!*

NEHANDA: I will not tell you that it is I, Nehanda the Spirit that battled wicked missionaries and criminal colonizers out of this here Zimbabwe, Zambia, Botswana, even before your grandfathers were boys.

I will not tell you that the white missionaries came and I said to my people, "Don't be afraid of them as they are only traders. Take a black cow to them and say this is the meat with which we greet you."

(Nehanda swallows hard.) But, why are these garments red, like those of one treading the winepress? Why are these garments red? *Nditaurire aniko!*

The blood of my children has *ngozi*; the blood of my children has unwanted spirits since mine was spilled. That *ngozi* will return to where it came from; it will return to the hands of the white missionary. Back to sender, back to sender.

(Tears well up in Nehanda's eyes.)

For they poured our blood on the ground, I will tell you this. *Ndichakutaurira.* My bones must rise again to avenge you. My bones will rise in the spirit of war. They will sing war songs with the harsh fire of battle. They will conjure new war songs and fight on until the shrines of the land of their birth are respected once more.

Scene 9: Epiphany/Let Them Eat Cake

Mama and Papa are getting ready for church, dressing in their colorful Sunday best. Mama places a cake on the table. It looks white from the outside because of the icing, but the cake itself is red, as we will find out. Mama has it out because she intends to give the cake to the homeless children at church.

MAMA: I am just saying that there is nothing sacred about our borders.

PAPA: You keep disturbing my ears with this idea. Anyhow, we have been at this talk of ancestors for hours.

(He notices the cake on the table.)

Is that the ruined cake you are going to give to the homeless children?

MAMA: Yes. Too much vanilla essence.

(She stares at the cake for a couple of beats and then quickly peeps through the curtain. She hears the sound of the neighbor's gate opening.)

Look at this silly woman next door basking in the sun like she owes me nothing. Since her party is finished, when is she going to return my pots? Actually, you know what? She can eat them.

PAPA: *(Deep sigh.)* So, how do you mean? About borders?

MAMA: *Ao!* Who drew them?

PAPA: Europeans, certainly.

MAMA: Why did they draw them?

PAPA: To organize our society. Do you not see how —

MAMA: No! When did you become dull? They were drawn up to serve European greed! They cut up this land between themselves like... like a cake!

(She begins to furiously gouge out hunks of the cake with her bare hands to illustrate this point. We see the redness of the cake.)

Take this piece, Belgium! *Ah merci bien.* Take this piece, Britain! Long live the Queen. Here, Portugal! *Aluta bloody continua.* Here, France! Here, Germany! Here! Here!

(Her husband watches without speaking. Mama then grabs a white cotton swab to wipe her hands. The red of the cake looks bloody on her hands and on the cloth. In silence she puts the cloth away and,

still in silence, snatches a piece of fried beef from the fridge.)

Ah, this maid! Even simple beef she cannot fry.

PAPA: Hmm... What a shame that we are headed for church. All these feelings you are having would go very well with chardonnay.

MAMA: Boemo makes sense, my husband. These countries are imaginary. The borders split apart ethnic groups and families. Even the word "tribe" is wrong, like Boemo said.

PAPA: Are you ready?

MAMA: *(Peeping through the curtain.)* This foolish woman says she cannot afford pots yet she can afford all this Brazilian hair to put on her head!

PAPA: Are you ready to leave for church, my wife?

MAMA: I should be able to claim the ancestral land our people roamed. Where are my earrings? Did you see my earrings, *rraabo*?

PAPA: Right there on the shelf.

MAMA: Thank you. Where is that boy? Let us go. We are going to miss church, *kana. Ei*, my husband, I cannot shake the feeling that the boy is right. These new ideas do not touch me right, but surely shared ancestors are more important than borders?

(Contemplatively.)

Should we even be worshiping in a congregational church?

PAPA: Let us not be radical, my wife.

MAMA: *(Aside.)* Hmm... I suppose that one does not tell a deaf person that war has broken out.

(Sincerely.) I do find these realizations uncomfortable, but

they are very seductive ideas.

Where is he?

PAPA: Boemo! Boemo! Come downstairs, we are going.

Scene 10: 1985

BOEMO: I was born plump and healthy in 1985, the year that the first HIV/AIDS case was recorded in Botswana. I am of the first generation that has never experienced an HIV-free Botswana.

In 1985, other countries like Uganda had been battling AIDS for several years—fiercely, fearfully, and hopefully. Naturally we looked to Uganda for strategies on how to combat AIDS. Ugandans had successfully used music and theater arts like puppetry to inform the young and old and the infection rates were declining. We, too, wanted to use arts to sprinkle information everywhere on our native land.

Therefore, as I was growing up in Botswana, the only African languages of AIDS activism—both visually and musically—were Ugandan. Uganda's hero, activist-musician Philly Bongole Lutaaya became our hero in Botswana as well. Serious times had arrived and we lamented losses big and small. Ten-year-old children recited AIDS poems in school.

(Recites an AIDS poem, almost as an aside.)

you wreck us with your might/ you make pain rain in our eyes/ malome's sniffles before an open casket/ his son, a *lekolwane*, fine boy gone too soon/ what shall we call you? *phamo-kate! mogare! bolwetse!*/ the sour yellow smell of hospital disinfectant for a hospital full of the infected/ shall we call you AIDS?

(Returns to the story of Philly Lutaaya.)

Just as AIDS has been a part of my Motswana experience, so has been Lutaaya's legacy, from five or six African countries away.

Scene 11: Philly Lutaaya

Philly begins to sing his Luganda hit song,"Diana." A cough stops him and after a long pause he speaks.

PHILLY LUTAAYA: *Gwe wange, era gwe gwenalonda. Nebwekiribakki no no, Sirikuleka. Kanjatule mu maaso ga bangi, Gwe wange era nze wuwo.*

Oba bwaavu, oba nno bwe bugagga. Nabeera nga naawe, kuba gwe-gwenalonda, Okufa kwe kulitwawula, gwe wange era nze wuwo.

Tuyambagane nga, Diana wulira olwalero, Lekka nkukuume, nga naawe Diana bwonkuuma, Nakulonda mubangi, Diana

babirye omulongo wo wo, Lekka nkutwaare maama ewange omutima gumbeere munteeko mwattu mweenya nze ndabbe akazigo, tambula ndabbe ebitumbwe, Simanyi nno bambi wotoli Diana ndibeera wa? Simanyi obiwulila Diana njazika ku matuugo, Akazigo mu manyo bwoseka mu oti mpulira nfiira wo,lekka nkutwaare mama ewange, nkakasa oja kweyagala.

(A coughing fit prevents Philly from finishing the song.)

I always tell myself: "Phillip, you may have traveled the world, but don't ever forget that you are African. You must be very proud of being African. Always, wherever you may go, identify yourself as a true African who knows that we are the sons and daughters of our grandfathers who labored for our glory and honor. Our dignity."

For the short time I have to live in this world, I want to lend a hand to fellow Ugandans who are fighting AIDS. I want to inform people. I will be the first prominent Ugandan, first African to declare that I have AIDS, to give AIDS a face.

(Pause.)

Furthermore, at this time, when our young Uganda nation is fighting to reconstruct herself, it needs all of us, including the sick and disabled. There must be no feeling of giving up. We must fight with all possible means to the last day. As a musician and writer, I regret that many songs, ideas, and sounds will never be heard. My work is nearly finished, but I promise that I will go on working with double the effort to see that I do all I can to serve you, Uganda. For me, there won't be any raising of the white flag to AIDS. The hunter in pursuit of an elephant does not stop to throw stones at birds; I will die fighting. For God and my country!

Scene 12: Itore Gape
("Re-dream Yourself" in Setswana)

Boemo is writing and thinking aloud…

BOEMO: I want to believe that a common ancestry is what binds us as Africans. I often imagine a common ancestor holding all Africans fiercely and warmly inside her womb. But we do not know that history, that womb. We are orphans. Bitter, broken, and beggarly orphans.

Our history of victories, intelligence, and organization has been successfully erased and replaced with sad fictions of—to borrow my dad's phrase—things tumbling into rough weather.

Years ago when I was a law student at Oxford, I met Africans from all over the continent. My three best friends were from Swaziland, Namibia, and Chad. It was sad, almost bitter, how little we knew of our common histories. Instead of history we bonded through common failures. We laughed at the spoils of the colonial attack. We ridiculed our cartoonish dictators covered in gold jewelry. We got drunk and painted pictures of our women who bleach their dark skin until it is orange. We imitated self-important and bureaucratic government employees.

(Laughs, almost maniacally.)

I believe it was Nietzsche who said, "Perhaps I know best why it is man alone who laughs; he alone suffers so deeply that he had to invent laughter."

Scene 13: The Way Things Should Be

Gulubani household. Mama just arrived home from work. Papa is already home.

MAMA: *Ei!* This heat. It has been curling around my neck all day. How was your day, my husband?

PAPA: Quite fine. I went to Parliament today and met with other MPs. We are trying to organize a petition to give us a salary increase.

MAMA: Let us hope it goes through this time.

PAPA: *(Kissing her on the cheek.)* How was yours, my wife?

MAMA: The usual. I had to refer a lot of people to the right offices. I never understood why everyone comes to us for inquiries. We are only the Office of the Ombudsman. We do not handle funerals for crying out loud.

PAPA: Funerals? What happened today?

MAMA: This man came in today just before tea break. I almost did not help him. Who comes just before tea break with many questions?

PAPA: So he wanted help with a funeral?

MAMA: Well, he wanted to bury a family member in a place that is not designated burial land. I told him to come back after lunch and he started talking about incompetence in the workplace. Then I pulled out my nail polish and ignored him. But he would not leave! He ranted and finally I told him *quickfastandinahurry* that before he can get burial space in that area, you have to fill out a pink form and sign your name in block capitals. You can get the form by first going through that door. You keep going straight, turn left and right and left again and there you will see a guard and you can ask him for office number 15, because our doors are not labeled. And then after that you take the body to the mortuary and come back next week. You have to make color photocopies of your *Omang* on 20 by 10 centimeters type of paper and take it to the police station to get them certified.

PAPA: Yes, of course. Why was he being a nincompoop? I tell you, things are all tumbling into rough weather.

(Pours two glasses of scotch. He hands one to his wife and takes a sip of his.)

MAMA: Well, that is not even the end of it. He started asking for the Director and I told him *quickfastandinahurry* that the Director is attending an international conference in Bangkok, Thailand. Then he asked for the Deputy Director and I told him that the Deputy Director is on sabbatical leave in the Okavango pondering the impact of HIV on the economy.

PAPA: Yes.

MAMA: But he went on to ask for the Minister himself! I was so annoyed that I could have burned those dreadlocks right off his foolish head! But being the Christian woman that I am, I still told him that the Minister is in Francistown as part of a working committee on how to manage youth with HIV/AIDS. I finally asked him what he wanted with those bosses that he could not tell me! At that moment I was almost twitching with annoyance. He wanted reimbursement for his deposit. Imagine! I told him point blank: our office does not deal with cases of reimbursement. You will need to talk to the mayor of Gaborone—go across the street!

PAPA: People do not know the respectful way things should be done anymore. It vexes me.

MAMA: Yes, me too!

(Takes a sip of her scotch.) Where is our son? Is he back from Parliament also?

PAPA: Yes. He is upstairs. I think he is drafting something. He is meeting with his constituents tomorrow. I am just pleased that he is working on something other than that bloody memoir.

MAMA: I say, the boy may be cantankerous with his ideas but he works hard for sure. My husband, you should talk to your people and make him a Cabinet Minister.

PAPA: We cannot rush a strategy, my wife. As my late father liked to say, "No strategy, no dynasty."

(He kisses her. They smile happily.)

Scene 14: All These People

BOEMO: I am formed of the Tswana people who ruled the land between the Okavango and the Vaal rivers. I am formed of the Kalangas ba-ka Nswazwi, of Mujaji the Rain Queen. I am formed of migrants who left Europe to find a new home on our native land. Whatever their own actions, they remain, part of me. In my veins courses the blood of the Malay slaves who came from the East. Their proud dignity informs my bearing, their culture a part of my essence. The stripes they bore on their bodies from the lash of the slave master are a reminder embossed on my consciousness of what should not be done.

Being part of all these people, and in the knowledge that none dare contest that assertion, I shall claim that I am an African and I am a Motswana.

I publish this memoir in honor of my loving parents, Zibanani and Cecilia Gulubani, who never knew that I could hear their drunken conversations about me from upstairs. I love you, Mom and Dad. And may you both rest in peace.

Botswana, re-imagine yourself.

THE END

ABOUT DONALD MOLOSI

Donald Molosi is a classically-trained actor and award-winning playwright. He holds an MA in Performance Studies from UCSB, a Graduate Diploma in Classical Acting from LAMDA, and a BA in Political Science and Theatre from Williams College.

Molosi is featured in *A United Kingdom*, opposite Golden Globe and Emmy award nominee David Oyelowo and Oscar nominee Rosamund Pike. The film depicts the marriage of Prince Seretse Khama and Ruth Williams in the 1940s and the uniting of the people of Botswana.

Molosi divides his time between Botswana and the United States.

ABOUT THE MANTLE

The Mantle publishes emerging critics, writers, and intellectuals in the arts, international affairs, literature, and philosophy. We foster discourse with a global audience through critiques, essays, fiction, and interviews. We pay close attention to voices with limited exposure in their home countries and the English language, as well as individuals experiencing censorship. Read essays on our online magazine at www.mantlethought.org and explore our print and ebook titles at www.mantlebooks.com.